CW01064540

Original title:
The Creative Challenge

Copyright © 2024 Book Fairy Publishing
All rights reserved.

Editor: Theodor Taimla
Author: Meelis Maurus
ISBN HARDBACK: 978-9916-763-80-3
ISBN PAPERBACK: 978-9916-763-81-0

Dance of Thoughts

In the quiet of the night,
When the world is fast asleep,
Ideas take their flight,
From the mind, they gently seep.

They swirl and twirl in glee,
Like dancers on a stage,
An endless, vibrant sea,
Forever turning the page.

Imaginations play and blend,
Creating visions, clear and bright,
In this waltz, there's no end,
To the magic of the night.

Hidden Genius

In shadows, brilliance hides,
Away from prying eyes,
Within the soul, abides,
A genius in disguise.

Ideas grow in silence,
With whispers, not applause,
Through patience and defiance,
It carves its own great cause.

One day the world will know,
The light within that shone,
From darkness, it will flow,
A genius fully grown.

Mind's Canvas

A canvas pure and vast,
Awaits the painter's touch,
Mind's colors moving fast,
Creating worlds as such.

Dreams and thoughts collide,
In strokes both bold and fine,
No boundaries to confide,
In this abstract design.

Imagination's flight,
Turns blankness into gold,
Art from the depths of night,
A masterpiece unfolds.

Boundless Imagination

Across infinite skies,
The mind begins to soar,
Through realms that mystify,
Where dreams forever pour.

No chains to bind its course,
No limits to constrain,
Imagination's force,
Ignites the wild terrain.

Through this endless expanse,
New worlds begin to spin,
In boundless, magic dance,
Where every thought's akin.

Mosaic of Thought

In the quiet of the mind, a mosaic forms,
Fragments of dreams, ideas in swarms.
Colors vibrant, each piece a lore,
Patterns unseen, an infinite store.

Whispers weaving, a tapestry bright,
Stars of insight guiding the night.
Intricate dances in the cerebral fog,
Rhythms of reason through the mental bog.

Under the surface, currents deep,
In silence profound, secrets seep.
Thoughts colliding in a wondrous tide,
Mosaic of thought, a journey inside.

Prism of Innovation

Beneath the surface where shadows play,
Visionary sparks light up the way.
Ideas refract in a prism of light,
Innovation glows, piercing the night.

Boundaries dissolve in creative streams,
Shaping the future with daring dreams.
Every spectrum of possible minds,
In the prism's embrace, invention finds.

Origin of change, a clandestine gem,
Bold and free in the creator's realm.
Prism of innovation, continuum bright,
Crafting tomorrow with radiant might.

Dreams Unveiled

Beyond the veil where whispers dwell,
Dreams unfurl in a boundless swell.
Visions vivid in a tapestry spun,
In moonlit realms where future's begun.

Ephemeral threads of hope and grace,
Weaving wonder in a cosmic space.
Follow the paths where mysteries lead,
Dreams unveiled, prophecies freed.

In the heart of night, truths arise,
Guided by starlight in endless skies.
Navigate the unknown, courage untailed,
In a world anew where dreams are unveiled.

Kaleidoscope of Creation

Spinning in a realm of vibrant hues,
Creation dances, ever-changing views.
Fragments form in a shifting scope,
Patterns merge in a kaleidoscope.

In each turn, a universe anew,
Infinite wonders in a prism's cue.
Colors blend in harmony grand,
Artistry shaped by an unseen hand.

Endless designs in a cyclic play,
Crafted pieces in a brilliant array.
Kaleidoscope of creation's delight,
A symphony born in the purest light.

Dreamcatcher's Quest

Beneath the moonlit, silver crest,
A path to dreams, a whispered quest.
Through windswept fields, the stars attest,
A journey to the heart's behest.

With every footstep, shadows yield,
As secrets in the night are sealed.
The dreamcatcher with webs revealed,
Holds stories long since unwheeled.

In twilight's glow, the spirits weave,
A tapestry of hopes perceived.
The nightingale sings, though hearts may grieve,
For dreams pursued are dreams achieved.

Forging Creativity

In the forge of thought, ideas blaze,
A molten flow of dawn's first rays.
From embers bright, the mind doth craze,
To shape anew from life's displays.

An anvil sharp, where visions meet,
The hammer falls in rhythmic beat.
With every strike, sparks dance and fleet,
Creating forms from shadows' sheet.

The artist's hand, with steadfast grace,
Invokes the muse in timeless space.
A masterpiece in every trace,
Forged in the fire of a soulful place.

Poetic Inventiveness

In the quiet hush, where muses sing,
Lies the seed of thought, awaiting spring.
With every word, new worlds it brings,
A symphony from a silent string.

Rhythms dance in cascades bright,
Echoes of the day and night.
Through verse and rhyme, they take their flight,
Painting dreams in purest light.

The poet's pen, a wand of gold,
Transforms the tales both young and old.
As stories rich and lyrics bold,
Unfolding wonders yet untold.

Sculpting Wonders

With hands that shape the formless clay,
Creators mold the break of day.
In every curve and line, we say,
A silent homage to the ray.

The chisel's kiss, a gentle breeze,
Reveals the forms the eye perceives.
From marble's heart, such dreams do seize,
Creating spells that time reprieves.

In stone and wood, the essence lies,
Of earth and sky, of low and highs.
Through sculpted wonders, soul replies,
To whisper truths without disguise.

Poignant Imaginings

In shadows deep where echoes dance,
Lost whispers speak of bygone chance.
A tear-streaked moon, its silver haze,
Reflects the sorrow of past days.

In dreams, the heart finds ache anew,
A wound reopened, old yet true.
Memories play in silent streams,
Haunted by what-never-seems.

A fragile hope, a distant gleam,
Fades into the twilight's seam.
Yearning fills each tender breath,
An elegy to love's soft death.

Imaginative Crescendo

Colors burst against the night,
Stars ignite in pure delight.
Waves of wonder, dreams take flight,
In realms beyond our finite sight.

A symphony of endless hues,
Mingle in the twilight's muse.
Imagination's tones arise,
Conducted through the boundless skies.

Each note a thread of vivid dreams,
Interwoven with moon's beams.
Universe in vibrant spree,
Choreographed in harmony.

Innovator's Flight

With wings of thought, the mind ascends,
To realms where possibility blends.
To mold a vision, pure and true,
In skies of infinite azure blue.

A spark ignites the fervent soul,
Ideas crafted seek their goal.
Through challenges, with fervent might,
Inventors carve their path to light.

On winds of change, their dreams unfurl,
A revolution shapes the world.
Bound to progress, day and night,
They chase the call of innovation's flight.

Boundless Generation

In hearts where dreams and visions swell,
A future's tale begins to tell.
Boundless hope in every hand,
We pave a bridge to promised lands.

Through perseverance, paths align,
Each step a testament, a sign.
Together weaving destiny,
We script our endless legacy.

Seeds of wonder, deeply sewn,
In fertile minds, these truths are known.
Generation bound by endless sky,
To dream, to reach, and rise up high.

Whispers of Inspiration

In the quiet hush of dawn,
Ideas begin to form,
Whispers softly drawn,
Through a mental storm.

Visions start to shimmer,
In the morning light,
Each thought a glimmer,
Of creative flight.

Echoes from the heart,
Speak in gentle tones,
Urging us to start,
Building on these stones.

A muse's soft caress,
Leads us to creation,
Inspiration's dress,
Born of contemplation.

Dreams take shape and rise,
Fuelled by fervent will,
On wings of the wise,
The mind is never still.

Brushstrokes of Genius

A canvas pure and white,
Awaits a master's hand,
Colors burst to light,
As dreams start to expand.

With strokes so bold and free,
A vision comes to life,
In hues of destiny,
Born from inner strife.

Textures weave and blend,
Stories yet untold,
Lines begin to bend,
Artistry unfolds.

Passion takes its toll,
On the artist's soul,
Imprints on the whole,
A genius' role.

Each brushstroke tells a tale,
In the silent symphony,
Of efforts that prevail,
In creativity's spree.

Symphony of Ideas

Ideas start to dance,
In a harmonious flow,
Like a trance,
A river in full glow.

Notes of thought align,
In perfect melody,
Each thread so fine,
Woven seamlessly.

Harmony of minds,
Across endless sea,
The future finds,
Possibility.

Concepts intertwine,
In a grand ballet,
Each one a sign,
Of a hopeful day.

A symphony resounds,
In the orchestra of night,
Where pure thought abounds,
And dreams take flight.

Colorful Musings

A palette rich and bright,
Pours onto the mind,
A spectrum of light,
In thoughts we find.

Colors start to speak,
In hues so bold,
Their stories are unique,
And seek to unfold.

Each shade a feeling,
Each tint a vibe,
The soul revealing,
Where colors imbibe.

Blending and mixing,
In the heart's own art,
No longer affixing,
One single part.

A world painted anew,
In the hues of thought,
Each view in the brew,
Of the colors sought.

Unbound by Conformity

Whispers of the wild winds,
Dance upon the sea,
Breaking chains of tethered thoughts,
Setting spirits free.

Colors of the untamed skies,
Blend in waves of light,
Painting stories never told,
Beyond the mortal sight.

Echoes of forgotten dreams,
Resonate so clear,
In a world where voices cry,
Freedom from their fear.

Paths that twist in mystery,
Unknown and unplanned,
Lead the heart to venture forth,
Into a liberated land.

Steps unbound by rigid lines,
Follow where they may,
In the realm of boundless minds,
Conformity gives way.

Tapestry of Ideas

Threads of thought in endless weave,
Craft a world so wide,
Where every pattern interlaced,
Inspires the hearts to guide.

From whispers of forgotten lore,
To echoes of the now,
Each idea a perfect stitch,
Beneath the thinker's brow.

Colors blend in vibrant hues,
In a canvas of the mind,
Where imagination's hand,
Leaves no piece behind.

Visions grand and subtle schemes,
Entwine in silent grace,
Forming endless possibilities,
In a timeless space.

In the loom of human thought,
Where dreams and wisdom meet,
A living tapestry evolves,
In ideas, pure and sweet.

Sparks of Genius

In the quiet of the night,
When silence reigns supreme,
A spark ignites the darkest sky,
Awakens the unseen.

Brilliance, like a comet's blaze,
Cuts through clouds of doubt,
Illuminates the path ahead,
With creativity's shout.

In the cauldron of the mind,
Imagination brews,
A chemistry of inspiration,
With colors bright and hues.

Within the forge of pure thought,
Molten ideas mold,
Transforming dreams into form,
In visions bold and gold.

As the ember's flame persists,
Against the cloak of night,
Genius thrives on every spark,
Chasing infinite light.

Quest for Inspiration

Across the realms of dream and dust,
Where shadows whisper lore,
A seeker treads on paths unknown,
In search of something more.

Mountains high and valleys low,
Spell tales of ancient days,
Guide the heart with subtle signs,
In labyrinthine ways.

Stars that pierce the velvet night,
Illuminate the quest,
Their gleam ignites the dormant spark,
In every pilgrim's chest.

In the echoes of the past,
And songs of yet to be,
Inspiration hides its face,
In moments wild and free.

Till at last the soul finds peace,
In ideas fresh and true,
The quest for inspiration ends,
In the beauty of the new.

Eloquent Artistry

In strokes of hue, the canvas weaves,
A tale of dreams, of heart believes.
Brushes dance in silent song,
Where colors merge, and souls belong.

Each line a whisper, soft yet bold,
Unveiling stories never told.
Textures speak in varied tone,
Crafting worlds where minds are sown.

Shapes and shadows, light embraced,
Masterpiece, a life untraced.
In the silence, beauty sings,
Echoes of imagined things.

Framed in timeless, gilded grace,
Artistry finds sacred space.
From the depths, a spark ignites,
In silent wonder, hearts take flight.

Whirlwind of Genius

Through minds alight, with fervor spins,
A whirlwind where the spark begins.
Ideas blaze in fervent flight,
Transforming dark into the light.

Each thought a tempest, wild and free,
An endless dance towards destiny.
Brilliance leaps from mind to page,
Unfolding in a fevered rage.

Creativity, a storm of gold,
In every breeze, new tales are told.
Genius swirls in vibrant streams,
Fueling dreams with rainbow beams.

In the chaos, order brews,
Crafting worlds with varied hues.
Cycles of the storm embrace,
The genius leaving timeless trace.

Endless Conceptions

In the cradle of the night,
Ideas dawn, swift takes flight.
Infinite the realms we find,
In the caverns of the mind.

Born from silence, thoughts entwine,
Crafting dreams from silver line.
Endless oceans, vast and deep,
Where imagination leaps.

Concepts tumble, wild and rare,
In the ether, floating there.
Seedlings of a grand design,
Sprouting in the heart's confine.

Infinite the visions cast,
Future, present, from the past.
Every spark a new creation,
Fueling boundless aspirations.

Envisioning Wonder

Through the veil of common day,
Lies a world, a hidden way.
Envisioning beyond the plain,
Where wonders dance, where dreams remain.

Eyes that see beyond the norm,
Find in shadows, magic born.
In the mundane, secrets lie,
Waiting for the probing eye.

Imagination's lantern glows,
Guiding where enchantment flows.
Every beam a hidden door,
To landscapes unexplored before.

Craft the wonder, shape the dream,
Draw from life's unending stream.
In the vision, essence pure,
Wonders found forevermore.

Splendor of Thoughts

In the quiet of the mind,
A spark begins to glow.
Whispers of a dream unwind,
In endless ebb and flow.

Ideas dance on beams of light,
Shimmering with grace.
In contemplations bright,
They find their sacred place.

Epiphanies like stardust fall,
On fields of pure reflection.
In every brilliant thought recall,
A universe in conception.

The splendor of thoughts displayed,
In intricate array.
A gallery of shadows swayed,
In hues of night and day.

Vision's realm, both vast and tall,
Where wisdom's echoes play.
In the splendor of thought's hall,
In timeless reverie, we stay.

Embodied Creation

From the pulse of depths unknown,
Forms arise in breath.
In the fabric of life sewn,
Defying time and death.

With hands of daring skill,
Matter is transformed.
Through the power of will,
Creation is performed.

Echoes of a heart's decree,
In shapes and contours cast.
Granite, wood, and filigree,
Fashioned through the past.

Art as flesh, and life as clay,
Born from dreams and reason.
In the twilight of the day,
Merges with each season.

Embodied thoughts to world belong,
In vision's grand reflection.
In each crafted song,
Lies the spark of pure perfection.

Crafting Eternity

In whispers of a timeless art,
Mortals shape the infinite.
With each stroke, they impart,
Impressions bold and delicate.

Through hands of ancient memory,
The eternal finds its form.
A legacy of symmetry,
In structures grand and warm.

Fragments of a cosmic breath,
Woven through all history.
Connections bridging life and death,
In eternal mystery.

Symbols carved in sacred stone,
Stories etched in tender hue.
Crafting time, where thoughts have flown,
In every shade and view.

Thus, the artisans of fate,
With moments gently sown.
Shape the boundaries and the gate,
To worlds that lie unknown.

Portals of Thought

From the recess of the mind,
Portals open wide.
Realms of insight we find,
In imagination's tide.

Through the gateway of a dream,
Mysteries unfold.
Past and present intertwine,
In stories yet untold.

Thoughts converge like rivers flow,
Streams to oceans deep.
Where knowledge's currents grow,
In ever-binding sweep.

Dimensions of awareness gleam,
In reflective beams.
Traversing through the mists unseen,
In consciousness's schemes.

Portals lead where reason bends,
To wonders scarcely known.
In the labyrinth thought extends,
New universes grown.

Design of Dreams

In the canvas of night, dreams do unfurl,
Soft whispers of hope, vivid and curled.
Silhouettes of wonder, shadows trace,
A journey embarked in a boundless space.

Colors blend, in twilight's embrace,
Patterns weave a timeless grace.
Through mazes of thought, unseen streams,
Flows the wondrous design of dreams.

Celestial lights cast their gentle beams,
Unveiling realms of ethereal themes.
Each star a story, each gleam a glance,
Invoking reverie, a mystic dance.

Mysteries bloom in the silent night,
Guiding hearts with a phantom light.
From ashes of dusk, bright visions rise,
Crafting new worlds in sleeping skies.

Aesthetic Ventures

We sail on seas of colors bright,
In the dawn of ideas' light.
Beauty beckons, horizons wide,
An odyssey on the aesthetic tide.

Textures whisper, patterns call,
In this boundless artistic sprawl.
Each brushstroke, a new frontier,
Unveiling wonders, far and near.

Through labyrinths of form we tread,
Crafting visions from golden thread.
Shapes and hues in harmonious blend,
In endless dances, journeys wend.

Sculpting dreams in clay and stone,
Finding life in the lifeless bone.
Art transcends in ventures bold,
A tale of beauty yet untold.

Creative Alchemy

From void to form, the magic flows,
In endless loops, ideas glow.
Through alchemy of mind and heart,
Creation thrives as dreams impart.

Thoughts ignite in fervent flames,
Transforming whispers into names.
Elements merge in passion's fire,
Birthing wonders, crafting desire.

Potions stir in cauldron's core,
Alchemy sings in silent lore.
Old to new, metals transmute,
Marvels arise from simplest root.

Every spark a novel spell,
Woven in the creative well.
Alchemy's touch on canvas bare,
Fills the world with radiant flair.

Roaring Ideas

In minds aflame with endless quest,
Ideas roar, unrest to unrest.
Thoughts combust in fervent flight,
Seeking truth through darkest night.

Echoes of the future call,
Boundless visions rise and fall.
In the storm of intellect's sea,
Ideas roar wild and free.

Midnight murmurs turn to shout,
Whirling winds of doubt and clout.
In the roar, new worlds take shape,
Creating tales of grand escape.

Untamed waters of the mind,
Roaring voices, undefined.
From chaos, order finds its face,
Harnessing dreams in furious pace.

Words in Flight

In the hush of twilight, words take wing,
Whispered dreams and secrets sing,
Across the sky, where stars ignite,
Poems soar in the velvet night.

Echoes of past, present, what might be,
Letters form constellations for all to see,
Ink becomes the night's long dance,
In the air, words take their chance.

Silent cries in the moon's embrace,
Verses float in timeless grace,
Through the ether, thoughts unbind,
Every breath, a story finds.

Invisible thread, binding souls,
Each word mends, each fragment consoles,
In the realm where shadows merge,
Language becomes the silent surge.

Hearts aflame with phrases bright,
Words in flight through the infinite night,
Beyond the horizon, where dreams alight,
A symphony of thought takes flight.

Trails of Creativity

In the core of silence, thoughts entwine,
On a path where sparks intertwine,
Unseen colors swirl and blend,
On trails where imagination sends.

Brush strokes of mind create the scene,
In abstract realms where visions lean,
Crafting realms from nothingness,
Weaves a universe of consciousness.

Footprints echo in the mind's domain,
In the landscape of the ethereal plane,
Infinite paths that twist and turn,
Flames of creation brightly burn.

Musing tendrils reach out wide,
Through cosmic waves, they swiftly glide,
Symbols, shapes in liquid form,
Creation's trail through quiet storms.

Fields of thought where inspirations rove,
Uncharted lands where spirit sows,
A pilgrimage of soul's delight,
Through trails of creativity, we take flight.

Crafting the Cosmos

In the delicate hands of timeless night,
Stars are woven with threads of light,
From chaos comes celestial forms,
A universe in quiet storms.

Galaxies spiral, old and new,
Crafting stories in cosmic hues,
Planets dance to silent tunes,
Under the gaze of ancient moons.

Nebulae blaze in colors bold,
History in their folds unfold,
Woven by hands unseen, unnamed,
Crafting the cosmos, unrestrained.

Each atom whispers tales of yore,
Infinite grains on an endless shore,
In the forge of time, they intertwine,
Creating realms, both dark and divine.

Crafted by forces vast and unseen,
A tapestry of dreams and in-betweens,
In the boundless, silent night,
Crafting the cosmos in endless flight.

Embrace the Unseen

In the stillness, mysteries reside,
Shadows where secrets may hide,
On the edge of light and unknown,
Whispers of realms yet to be shown.

Veils of the unseen gently part,
Revealing the magic at heart,
Beyond what eyes alone may view,
Lies a world both ancient and new.

To senses heightened, truths appear,
Through the silence, whispers clear,
In the depths where dreams unwind,
The unseen world's wonders we find.

Embrace the void, the space between,
Where reality and dreams convene,
In the dance of shadows, light unseen,
Truth and fantasy brightly gleam.

Through the veil, take gentle flight,
Into the realms of endless night,
In the unseen, our spirits find,
The endless realm of the boundless mind.

Harmony in Chaos

In maelstroms deep, where shadows dance,
A symphony unfolds by chance.
Blades of chaos twist and twine,
Crafting tunes both sharp and fine.

Harmony emerges, bright and clear,
In turmoil's grasp, it sheds all fear.
Notes of discord interlace,
To form a gentle, sweet embrace.

Storms within the mind do whirl,
Creating butterflies that swirl.
From the chaos, beauty shifts,
Transforming rifts to cosmic gifts.

Order hides within the storm,
Guiding hands to reshape form.
An artful blend of wild and tame,
In chaos lies the perfect frame.

Patterns rise from disarray,
In chaos, true harmonies lay.
With each strum of cosmic fire,
Chaos breeds the heart's desire.

Visionary Twists

Across the dreams of worlds unknown,
The visionary seed is sown.
Twists and turns in future's light,
Guide the way through endless night.

Paths uncharted by the eye,
Reveal horizons vast and high.
In the shadows of the mind,
Possibilities unwind.

Stars align in novel forms,
Ideas birthed in cosmic storms.
Twists of fate blend to inspire,
Fueling hearts with boundless fire.

With each twist, a new dawn breaks,
Infinite the paths it makes.
Vision rides on wings of dreams,
Carving out those hidden beams.

Through the maze of thought and time,
Visionaries craft the sublime.
Twists of logic, bends of space,
Illuminate the human race.

Fusion of Minds

Two minds intertwine as one,
Bridging gaps, new dawns begun.
Fusion sparks a blazing flame,
Unites souls through shared aim.

Thoughts converge in brilliant light,
Ideas take their fated flight.
Boundaries blur, dissolve in grace,
Together they create a space.

Conversations weave and meld,
Stories shared, perspectives held.
In the fusion, wisdom's found,
Hearts and minds by love are bound.

Shared dreams paint a future vast,
Forging friendships meant to last.
Minds that blend in unity,
Craft a world of harmony.

In the fusion, limits break,
New horizons for hearts' sake.
Minds in union, hands entwined,
Together, they will surely climb.

Ode to Originality

To the soul that dares to be,
Unique, unfettered, wild, and free.
Original in thought and form,
A beacon in a world of norm.

Breaking molds with every breath,
Creating life from dying death.
With every stroke, a masterpiece,
Originality can't cease.

In the face of mimicry,
Stands the heart of mystery.
Crafting paths none dared to walk,
Speaking truths that others balk.

Each creation, bright and new,
Witness to a spirit true.
In the depths of self and mind,
Originality we find.

Celebrate the bold and rare,
Those who choose to always dare.
For in the light of their bright flame,
We find our courage, find our name.

Celestial Inspiration

Beneath the stars, dreams softly flow,
Whispers of the night, a gentle glow.
Constellations cast their ancient lore,
Guiding hearts to seek, explore.

In twilight's veil, thoughts ascend,
Boundless skies, horizons blend.
Galaxies weave stories bright,
In cosmic dance, souls unite.

Heavens hum with melodies pure,
Echoes of silence, vast and sure.
Planets spin in rhythmic grace,
Timeless beauty, endless space.

Across the universe's bound,
Wisdom in the silence found.
Stars ignite the paths unknown,
In their light, we're not alone.

Infinite dreams in midnight's gaze,
Celestial realms, eternal maze.
Inspiration from the spheres,
Guides us through the endless years.

Pioneering Insights

Through uncharted realms we strive,
Curiosity keeps the spark alive.
Questions lead to paths untamed,
In search of truths, the unknown claimed.

Innovators light the way,
Turning night into hopeful day.
With each step on the boundless ground,
New horizons are profoundly found.

Discovery in every glance,
Ideas born from happenstance.
Crafting futures brave and new,
Pioneering vision through and through.

Challenges met with steadfast grace,
Inventing strides at their own pace.
Mind and spirit ever bold,
Pioneers of thought, hearts of gold.

Insight found in every turn,
Knowledge waits for those who yearn.
Boundless questing lights the night,
Guided by pioneering insight.

Indelible Creativity

Canvas whispers tales untold,
Sculpting dreams with fingers bold.
Infinite blooms from humble seeds,
Creativity fulfills our needs.

Colors dance in vibrant play,
Imprints left in each array.
Brushes sweep, emotions soar,
Expressions rich, forever more.

Music's chords in hearts entwine,
Rhythms pulse with endless line.
Verses speak with voices clear,
Harmonies that we hold dear.

Words like rivers, thoughts they flow,
Stories weave where imaginations grow.
Crafting worlds within our mind,
Indelible traces left behind.

Art transcends the bounds of time,
In every form, and every rhyme.
Creativity's everlasting flame,
A legacy we proudly claim.

Eternal Muse

In shadows deep and light immense,
The muse whispers, calm and tense.
Echoes of a timeless song,
In every heart, she plays along.

Whispers of an age-old lore,
Muse's touch, we yearn for more.
Infinite source of wonder's grace,
In every art, we find her trace.

In dreams, she softly lingers near,
In every thought, she's crystal clear.
Guiding hand and vision bright,
Inspiration through the night.

Her essence in the wind's soft sigh,
In every glance, a secret lie.
Eternal spark in fleeting glance,
In her embrace, we find the chance.

Boundless well where poets drink,
In her depths, we cease to sink.
Eternal muse, our guiding star,
In her light, we'll journey far.

Harmonious Inventions

Waves of creation, boundless and bright,
In every idea, an infinite light.
From shadows of doubt, pure wonder ascends,
Crafting new worlds where the mind transcends.

Tools in our hands, awakened to dream,
Fields of potential, as vast as they seem.
In the heart of the cosmos, thoughts come alive,
A melody merging, where visions thrive.

Echoes of genius, in symphonic tide,
Concepts are born, with nothing to hide.
Through bonds of brilliance, unity's sphere,
The echoes of harmony, perfectly clear.

Ephemeral moments, captured in time,
Invention through whispers, a silent rhyme.
Together we sculpt, an infinite thread,
Harmonies interwoven, brilliance widespread.

Symphony of Ideas

Notes of thought in a resonant blend,
In the chamber of minds, new arcs ascend.
Connected by threads unseen, yet strong,
Ideas flow, a continuous song.

From whispers of inspiration, sparks ignite,
A canvas of dreams, in symphonic flight.
Every notion a wordless refrain,
Building a skyline from thoughtful terrain.

A dance of neurons, electric and free,
In the grand orchestra of creativity.
Each mind a player, each thought a chord,
Resonating truth in a shared accord.

Ideas converge in a grand travail,
Crafting a tale where visions sail.
Together we shape the world's design,
A symphony of ideas, forever entwined.

Whispers of Imagination

In the silence of night, soft voices play,
Whispers of dreams in delicate array.
Carving new paths where shadows meet light,
Imagination rises, in glorious flight.

With every breath, the cosmos expands,
Stories unspoken in tender hands.
Through the veil of reality, visions appear,
Painting new wonders, bright and clear.

Silent musings from the heart's deep core,
Transcending the mundane forever more.
Each whisper a seed, in fertile ground,
From stillness to grandeur, so profound.

A touch of magic in every thought,
Worlds within worlds tenderly wrought.
The whispers of imagination take flight,
Writing new chapters in endless delight.

Dance of the Muse

Beneath the moon, a muse does weave,
Dreams awakened, in twilight's eve.
A dance of shadows, of light and grace,
Inspire the heart, their steps embrace.

With every turn, new visions arise,
Crafting wonders before our eyes.
In hues of gold and shades of blue,
The dance of the muse, eternally true.

Whispers in silence, movements in air,
Ideas take form with tender care.
In every step, a story unfolds,
A tale of inspiration, brightly told.

Through time and space, the muse does glide,
In the realm where dreams reside.
A dance of beauty, of endless muse,
Capturing hearts with gentle ruse.

Beyond the Blueprint

In sketches bold and lines defined,
A world of wonder lies refined.
Blueprint shadows cast their tale,
Dreams unfurling beyond the veil.

With compass, chart the stars above,
Engineers of dreams and love.
From thought to form, a bridge appears,
In the span of years and tears.

Crafted with a steady hand,
Silent whispers command,
Structures rise to kiss the sky,
A testament to those who try.

Steel and stone, in concert sing,
Every column, beam, and wing,
Beyond the page, a life anew,
A blueprint world for me and you.

In the heart of plans conceived,
Dreams are born and wars relieved,
Blueprints fade, but not their song,
In every hope, they linger strong.

Myriad of Dreams

In the twilight's gentle glow,
Dreams like rivers start to flow,
A tapestry of stars unfurled,
Embarking towards another world.

Shadows dance in moonlit beams,
Weaving threads of myriad dreams.
Every whispered wish and sigh,
Patterned in the midnight sky.

Glimpses of an untouched shore,
Behind the edge of sleep's closed door,
A realm where fantasies collide,
Infinite wonders coincide.

In the quiet, thought takes flight,
Traversing realms of endless night,
Each slumbered breath another key,
Unlocking dreams, setting them free.

Awake, we leave this mystic land,
Yet dreams linger, hand in hand,
Guiding us through hours of day,
In a myriad of dreams, we stay.

Awakening the Muse

In the stillness, thoughts arise,
Unseen hands that weave the skies,
Wisps of dreams to paper flow,
Awakening the muse we know.

Idle whispers, soft and sweet,
Gentle rhythms, heart's own beat,
From the shadows, verses spring,
Muse revived, let poets sing.

Inspiration flickers fast,
Holding moments that will last,
Muse's voice a guiding light,
Through the depths of darkest night.

Every stroke of pen a trace,
Capturing the muse's grace,
Words take form and open doors,
To her world, forever ours.

Awakening, she breathes anew,
Colors bright and visions true,
Muse, our ever-present guide,
Through her eyes, the world is wide.

Light Through Ink

Light through ink, the shadows play,
Tracing dreams in shades of gray,
Each line etched by hand and heart,
Crafting stories from the start.

Words arise like morning sun,
Drawing scenes where none begun,
In the glow of artist's flair,
Life reflected everywhere.

Ink and light, a mystic blend,
On this journey, worlds we send,
Through the dark and into dawn,
Narratives of hope are drawn.

From the pen, a lantern bright,
Shines the truth through endless night,
In each stroke, a glimpse of soul,
Light and ink to make us whole.

Pages shimmer with their glow,
Written dreams in ebb and flow,
Bright as day or dark as coal,
Ink, the light that lights us all.

Inception of Wonder

In the silent dawn of waking dreams,
New horizons softly gleam.
Mysteries unfold their lore,
In the heart, a mystic door.

Whispers of a world untold,
Emerald valleys, hills of gold.
Every star a secret keeps,
In the night where wonder sleeps.

Wings of thought begin to soar,
From the mundane, we explore.
Within the deep and boundless skies,
Truths are born and wonders rise.

In the silence, stories form,
Inspiration, the norm.
Beneath the surface, worlds ignite,
In dreams emerge, eternal light.

Eyes awaken to the new,
Life's canvas painted with a hue.
Inception of a wonder bright,
A universe within, alight.

Threads of Brilliance

In the loom of time, a weave,
Threads of brilliance interleave.
Moments spun in light and shade,
Tapestries of grace displayed.

Patterns intricate and fine,
Colors blend, a grand design.
Every thread a voice, a spark,
Illuminating journey's arc.

Hands of fate in silent dance,
Guiding threads of happenstance.
In each weave, a story told,
Of courage, love, and hearts of gold.

In the fabric of our days,
Brilliance threads in myriad ways.
From the warp, a vision glows,
Infinite where fiber flows.

In the weave, our dreams unfold,
Touches of the cosmic mold.
Threads of brilliance, ever bright,
Weaving through the endless night.

A Stroke of Genius

In the mindscape, quiet still,
Ideas form with silent thrill.
A stroke of genius, bold and free,
Unlocks the realms of mystery.

From the void, a spark alights,
Igniting thoughts like starry nights.
Each concept, a beacon shines,
Tracing paths of grand designs.

Through the chaos, order peaks,
Creations born in daring streaks.
Wisdom pours from hands, from heart,
Artistry, where muses start.

Imagination paints the air,
With colors vibrant, visions rare.
A stroke of brilliance, bold and new,
Crafting wonders, world view.

In the silence, genius hums,
With every stroke, a new dawn comes.
Infinite, the journey spreads,
As strokes of light fill the heads.

Genesis of Art

From the void, a birth of light,
In the shadows, colors bright.
The genesis of art revealed,
In every brush, a truth concealed.

Canvas bare, awaiting dreams,
Motions flowing, rhythmic streams.
Each creation, breath of soul,
A universe in part and whole.

Minds engaged in fervent trance,
Crafting visions, circumstance.
Every hue and every line,
Bears a glimpse of the divine.

Hands in motion, heart in flight,
Crafting day and painting night.
Genesis in every stroke,
The dawn of art as muses spoke.

In the birth of every scene,
Worlds emerge, serene, unseen.
From the void and into sight,
The genesis of endless light.

Ideas Unleashed

In the quiet of night, thoughts take flight,
Whispers of wisdom, they shine so bright.
Dreams unfurl like sails on a quest,
Ideas unleashed, at their very best.

Beyond the horizon, where visions reside,
Boundless creativity, nowhere to hide.
Through realms of wonder, our minds shall soar,
Ideas unleashed, forever more.

Silent musings erupt like a storm,
Shattering norms, taking new form.
In the dance of creation, spirits are freed,
Ideas unleashed, planting the seed.

From the depths within, voices call,
Breaking chains, breaking walls.
Unveiling new worlds, through uncharted seas,
Ideas unleashed, riding the breeze.

Moments of magic, fleeting, yet vast,
Transforming the future, shaping the past.
In the heart's fire, they find their peace,
Ideas unleashed, their power won't cease.

Visionary Palette

In the artist's mind, colors collide,
Hues of passion, no place to hide.
Brush strokes of dreams on canvas wide,
A visionary palette, dreams can't deride.

From dawn's glow to twilight's embrace,
Vibrant visions in endless space.
In the spectrum of thought, they reside,
A visionary palette, the spirit's guide.

Shades of hope and tones of despair,
Each stroke a journey, rich and rare.
On this canvas, emotions abide,
A visionary palette, far and wide.

Through abstract realms, forms entwine,
Creation's pulse in every line.
In the gallery of the soul, they glide,
A visionary palette, pure, refined.

Textures of time, both old and new,
Infinite vistas come into view.
In the heart's gallery, eternities bide,
A visionary palette, forever dyed.

Luminary Thoughts

In the twilight glow, ideas ignite,
Stars of wisdom, burning so bright.
Guiding souls through the vast night,
Luminary thoughts, a radiant sight.

Eclipsing darkness, they spread the light,
In the mind's expanse, they take flight.
With clarity and purpose, shining clear,
Luminary thoughts, drawing near.

Silent yet profound, they illuminate,
Truths and insights they narrate.
Through the corridors of knowledge, they wend,
Luminary thoughts, with no end.

From the heart's depth, they ascend,
Infinite trails, they weave and blend.
In the realm of the profound, they reside,
Luminary thoughts, our guiding tide.

They bear the weight of timeless lore,
Opening mind's every door.
In their gleam, we find our peace,
Luminary thoughts, they never cease.

Imaginative Journeys

Beyond the mundane, where wonders reside,
Imagination's wings, in full stride.
Through landscapes of dreams, paths unfold,
Imaginative journeys, stories untold.

In realms unseen, thoughts intertwine,
Ephemeral worlds, both yours and mine.
Each step reveals a truth, a quest,
Imaginative journeys, at their best.

Oceans of wonder, mountains high,
In a sky of thoughts, they freely fly.
Through valleys of creativity, rivers wind,
Imaginative journeys, where we're aligned.

Castles of cloud and forests of light,
In this cosmos, day turns to night.
With each whisper, with each breath,
Imaginative journeys, defeating death.

In every corner, tales to be found,
Magic in silence, without a sound.
In this odyssey of the mind's delight,
Imaginative journeys, eternal flight.

Inventive Souls

In the crucible of night, dreams ignite,
Weaving wonders, reaching height.
Through stars they whisper, bold and bright,
Inventive souls take flight.

With every spark, new worlds arise,
An endless realm of brilliant skies.
From shadows deep, ideas untie,
Crafting realms of surprise.

Bold explorers, minds unfurled,
In the realms of thought, they're hurled.
Side by side, creation swirled,
Rendering a brand-new world.

Luminous seeds in fertile mind,
Where creativity's intertwined.
Minds so free, unconfined,
Discoveries for humankind.

In unity, their spirits blend,
To the boundaries, they'll extend.
Through the cosmos, messages send,
Inventive souls transcend.

Kaleidoscope of Thoughts

In the flux of colors, minds convene,
Threads of thought, a vibrant scene.
Each twist and turn, worlds serene,
A brilliant, ever-changing screen.

Ideas bloom in radiant spikes,
A kaleidoscope above all likes.
Through introspection, it strikes,
With potent hues, our psyche hikes.

Every shard, a notion pure,
Minds entwined, connections sure.
In the dance, all thoughts endure,
Wondrous patterns to assure.

Visions spin, a fluent arc,
In twilight's beam, stark and dark.
Kindled minds, a radiant spark,
In paths uncharted, they embark.

In resplendence, thoughts align,
Through the glass, their colors shine.
Paving paths by design,
A kaleidoscope, so divine.

Enchanted Innovations

In realms of wonder, magic starts,
Ideas forged from very hearts.
Through the veil, it imparts,
Enchanting minds, where wisdom charts.

Phantasmal dreams entwined with light,
Crafting marvels in the night.
With every dawn, the ideas take flight,
Enchanting visions take their height.

Wizards of thought, where futures bloom,
In the silence, abandon gloom.
Illuminating the darkened room,
Creating beyond time's tomb.

Sigils of ingenuity, drawn in sky,
Invention's whispers, passing by.
On wings of brilliance, they fly,
Innovations aiming high.

In mystic ways, ideas flow,
Through enchanted streams, they grow.
With every thought, the wonders show,
Innovations in a magic glow.

Poetic Fusions

In verses bound by rhythmic thread,
Poetic fusions twist and spread.
Through heartfelt whispers being said,
A tapestry of words is bred.

Metaphors in cadence dance,
Every line, a master's trance.
In poetic realms, hearts romance,
Lost in lyrical expanse.

Each stanza mirrors worlds anew,
In ink and dreams, their bond is true.
Fused in verses, bright as dew,
Poems birth ethereal view.

Metered echoes, harmony bright,
Finding solace in the night.
In every rhyme, a guiding light,
Woven fusions soaring heights.

Hearts and minds in rhythm blend,
Through the stanzas without end.
With every line, thoughts ascend,
Poetic journeys we commend.

Realm of Fantasies

In the realm where dreams reside,
Magic whispers on the breeze,
Wondrous tales of distant lands,
Where hearts and spirits sail with ease.

Moonlit rivers gently flow,
Carrying secrets yet untold,
Stars align to sketch the sky,
Glowing stories of the bold.

Forests deep with ancient lore,
Guarded by the elder trees,
Mystic creatures, unseen power,
Nature's hidden harmonies.

Wandering souls find solace here,
In landscapes richly woven,
Fate and chance entwined in dance,
Timeless truths by dreams are spoken.

Here lies the boundless, endless space,
Where wonder never sleeps,
In the realm of fantasies,
All is more than what it seems.

Ethereal Inventions

Within the mind's expansive sea,
Ideas shimmer, dreams take flight,
Crafted in the forge of thought,
Born from quiet, starry night.

Echoes of a brilliant spark,
Whispers from the cosmic winds,
Weave the threads of future worlds,
Where imagination never ends.

Intricate designs unfold,
Marvels wrought from vision's clay,
Shapes unseen, yet deeply felt,
In the ether they will play.

Innovations softly bloom,
Glimmers of the yet unknown,
Blueprints drawn by unseen hands,
Crafting realms to call our own.

Mysteries of the boundless mind,
Wondrous, weightless, light projections,
Ethereal paths converge, create,
Endless fields of pure inventions.

Dazzling Conceptions

From the spark of thought we weave,
Dazzling threads of pure design,
Patterns shine in radiant glow,
In the loom of dreams entwined.

Visions leap from silent minds,
Glimmering like morning dew,
Taking form in splendor bright,
Colored by imagination's hue.

Ephemeral yet striking true,
Fantasy and reason meld,
Grand creations bloom in light,
In hearts and minds forever held.

Each conception, bold and bright,
Kindles fire in the soul,
Illuminating pathways new,
Guiding us toward a fuller whole.

Behold the magic, see it spring,
Dazzling thoughts in full ascension,
Here, in realms of crafted sight,
Thrive our shining, grand conceptions.

Unfolding Brilliance

In the dawning light of thought,
Whispers bloom from shadows old,
Ideas burgeon, truths unveil,
In brilliance they unfold.

Glimpses of a brighter world,
Caught within the mind's embrace,
Unseen forces shape and turn,
Guiding hands to wisdom's grace.

Fleeting moments, crystal clear,
Echoes of forgotten light,
Reshape realms, once dimly seen,
Into vistas blinding bright.

Thoughts in radiant array,
Bursting forth like primal stars,
Carve new trails through time and space,
Breaking through creative bars.

Beams of insight, cutting through,
Mysteries now made plain and bold,
In this dance of light and thought,
All unfolds, the brilliance told.

Crafting Brilliance

In hands of artisans, wonders form,
Each stroke a promise, each cut a charm.
With patience, skill, and endless calm,
From raw to refined, gold from warm.

Ideas take shape, like morning dawn,
Bright inspirations, from dusk till dawn.
Intricate designs, on papers drawn,
Each masterpiece born, adorning lawn.

The forge of minds, a searing light,
Creation blooms, in darkest night.
In sweat and toil, hearts take flight,
Brilliance weaves, pure delight.

Metal and wood, in deft embrace,
Crafted by hand, in sacred place.
With every twist, a line of grace,
A living art, leaves lasting trace.

Tools of trade, in silent praise,
Mark the hours, turn the days.
Brilliance crafted, in subtle ways,
A timeless craft, forever stays.

Fantastical Realms

In realms where dragons soar the sky,
Mystic lands where legends lie.
Eldritch forests, fairies nigh,
Magic whispers, just nearby.

A castle's shadow, moonlit bright,
Echoes of the ancient night.
Wizards weave their spellbound sight,
Boundless dreams take eager flight.

Underneath the emerald sea,
Mermaids sing in harmony.
Cities lost, where time sets free,
Fantastical realms of mystery.

High atop the crystal peaks,
Eagles spy the realm that speaks.
People's hearts, where magic sneaks,
In every corner, intrigue reeks.

Mystic portals far and wide,
Secrets with their gateways hide.
Journeys paved by guardian guide,
In these realms, our souls abide.

Sculpted Imagery

Chiseling stone, a dance begins,
Soft whispers turn to lions' grins.
Every strike a tale akin,
The sculptor's heart, the soul therein.

Clay takes form, with tender touch,
Hands that mold, with love so much.
Figures rise, life's breath as such,
Touch of magic, gentle clutch.

Marble breathes in soft embrace,
Emerging forms take silent place.
In lines and curves, a hidden grace,
Sculpted stories, time does trace.

Wood is carved in intricate line,
Figures shaped from earthly vine.
Mortal hands with art divine,
Sculpted imagery, pure design.

In galleries, the statues stand,
Silent sentries, through the land.
Language of the heart in hand,
Sculpted dreams, forever planned.

Mind's Workshop

In the mind's vast workshop deep,
Ideas forge and secrets keep.
Crafted thoughts in silence seep,
In waking dream or slumbered sleep.

Blueprints drawn on mental page,
Schemes to build, or thoughts to gauge.
Every notion, a gilded cage,
To free the dreams or stage the stage.

Across neurons, signals race,
Connecting thoughts in swift embrace.
A tapestry of fervent chase,
Mind's workshop, boundless space.

Imagination's hammer falls,
Creating worlds within its walls.
From grand ideas to tales so small,
Workshop of mind, it scripts them all.

In quiet hours or bustling throng,
Mind's workshop hums, a ceaseless song.
Building ideas, so bright and strong,
A ceaseless forge, where dreams belong.

Nexus of Ideas

In the mind's vast expanse, ideas bloom,
A garden of thoughts in full array.
Connections spark in mental room,
Where day dreams dance in bright display.

Through paths unseen, they weave along,
A symphony of silent song.
Each notion, each unfurling spawn,
Builds bridges steady, wondrous, strong.

Across the chasms of the mind,
Through whispers of the unseen kind,
Ideas fuse and intertwine,
In patterns only hearts can find.

Woven Inspirations

Threads of thought in mindful weave,
Patterned tapestries we believe.
Colors, vibrant, rich, and bright,
Crafted by the soul's own light.

In moments still, the threads commence,
Creating worlds through thought's defense.
Looms of wonder, bound and spun,
Inspiration's work is never done.

Fingers trace the woven line,
Mapping out the grand design.
Through each stitch, new hopes climb,
Crafting stories of our time.

Harbor of Thoughts

Deep within the quiet mind,
A harbor safe from tempests' wind.
Thoughts find refuge, still and kind,
In the port where dreams begin.

Anchored deep beneath life's tide,
Moments, fleeting, here reside.
Whispers, gentle, reconvene,
In the harbor's calm serene.

Each reflection finds its place,
In the echoes of this space.
Harbor safe from worldly chase,
Thoughts return with gentle grace.

Exploration of the Mind

Vast expanse of inner space,
Journeys start without a trace.
Every thought a chance to find,
New horizons, undefined.

Through the corridors unseen,
Explorers of the mind convene.
Mapping out vast mental seas,
Gaining wisdom with each breeze.

Day and night, the quest unfolds,
Mysteries of self behold.
Charting paths through mental gold,
In the mind, we're free and bold.

Chasing the Muse

In twilight's gentle, calming hue,
Ideas bloom in whispers, true.
Through quiet night, the thoughts ensue,
As shadows dance, our dreams pursue.

A muse unseen, in darkness hides,
Imagination's secret guides.
From starry skies, inspiration rides,
The mind unfurls, and words collide.

We chase the muse, on fervent wing,
A song unseen, we hear it sing.
Within our hearts, a spark to cling,
In silent night, creations spring.

With dawn's first light, the visions fade,
Yet in our souls, impressions made.
The artist's hand, in starlight swayed,
Leaves echoes of the night's cascade.

Through day and night, the chase endures,
For in our hearts, the muse secures.
A poet's quest, forever pure,
In endless dreams, we find our cures.

Sparks of Creation

In moments brief, a spark ignites,
Transforming worlds in darkest nights.
With every thought, a flame alights,
Creation's dance, in soaring flights.

From void to life, with force it springs,
An artist's touch, on tender wings.
Through whispers soft, the vision clings,
And into being, beauty brings.

With steady hand, the canvas flows,
Each stroke a tale, as passion grows.
In twilight's light, inspiration glows,
And unseen realms, the artist knows.

The genesis of thought and fire,
In every heart, a burning pyre.
From chaos comes the mind's desire,
To shape the world with dreams entire.

In shadows cast by fleeting noon,
The seeds of thought begin to bloom.
Through endless night to crescent moon,
Creation's spark dispels the gloom.

Visionary Echoes

In quiet halls of thought, we tread,
Where echoes of the past are spread.
With every step, a future led,
By visions kept, our spirits fed.

The dreams we weave in silent hours,
Unveil the world's unseen towers.
In whispered night, the vision flowers,
A symphony of inner powers.

Through cryptic words our eyes convey,
The echoes of a distant day.
In night's embrace, our thoughts relay,
The traces of a brighter way.

The past's reflection, clear and true,
Illuminates our path anew.
In visionary echoes, through,
We find the sparks of what we'll do.

And as the echoes softly fade,
Their wisdom in our hearts is laid.
With newfound light, our paths are made,
By visions that our souls conveyed.

Inventive Horizons

On horizons vast, our dreams take flight,
In dawn's first blush, a canvas bright.
Imagination's pure delight,
Unfolds in hues of morning light.

In realms unknown, where thoughts transcend,
The limits break, new paths we send.
With every step, new worlds we mend,
In boundless skies where dreams extend.

The mind untamed, an endless sea,
Of possibilities yet to be.
From concept born, comes destiny,
In inventive dreams, we find the key.

By starlit glow, the hours we chase,
Inventing worlds through time and space.
Each fleeting thought, a form we trace,
In endless night, we find our place.

Through challenges that life may pose,
The inventive mind forever grows.
With every dawn, where light bestows,
The horizon shifts, as new winds blow.

Palette of Thought

In colors rich and shadows deep,
Ideas in vibrant spectrum sweep,
Brushstrokes dance, a painter's grace,
In mind's gallery, hues embrace.

Cerulean dreams of skies afar,
Amber glows like evening star,
Verdant fields with emerald views,
Palette of thought, endless hues.

Crimson passions set aflame,
Chartreuse whispers softly name,
Lavender breaths of twilight's sheen,
Canvas of thought, dreamer's scene.

Sienna tales of ancient sands,
Ochre warmth in open hands,
Azure waves on silent shores,
Thoughts poured out 'til nevermore.

Midnight black and ivory white,
Merge to craft the dawn's first light,
Spectrum bends, our minds explore,
Palette of thought, forevermore.

Crafting Dreams

With needle fine, and thread of gold,
In twilight's hush, our dreams unfold,
Each stitch a wish, each seam a prayer,
In fabric spun from midnight air.

Soft whispers weave in moonlit strands,
We craft our dreams with tender hands,
Patterns of hope in every fold,
Stories of futures yet untold.

Twilight looms with silver sheen,
Threads of thoughts by night unseen,
Shadows dance, a quiet gleam,
Crafting the contours of our dream.

Tapestry of hopes and fears,
Drawn in slumbers, stitched by years,
Fantasy's cloth, in sleep we mend,
Crafting dreams without an end.

Through the night our visions glide,
On woven paths of starry guide,
In morning's light, bright and clear,
Dreams we've crafted reappear.

Echoes of Innovation

In caverns deep where shadows play,
Inventive sparks light up the way,
Echoes of ideas, unconfined,
Reverberate within the mind.

Through ancient halls of thought we roam,
Seeking paths once left alone,
Innovation's whispers spread,
Fresh voices from the silence bred.

Skies of mind in lightning flash,
Vision clears in brilliant dash,
Concepts born in thunder's cheer,
Echoes ring as thoughts adhere.

Imagination's boundless flight,
Soaring high in endless night,
Echoes form and reshape bounds,
Innovation in silent sounds.

Era's tide in moonlit gleam,
Carries forth each novel dream,
Symphony of future's call,
Echoes of innovation, free for all.

Sculpting Silence

On marble vast, where whispers fade,
Quiet hands in shadows wade,
To carve the stillness, pure and white,
In blocks of silence, soft and light.

Chisel strokes in twilight's glow,
Crafting echoes, soft and low,
In calm repose, the form appears,
Shaped by dreams and silent tears.

Through the hush of dark and dawn,
Sculpting calm with art withdrawn,
In every curve, a silent plea,
In every fold, tranquility.

Statues rise with quiet grace,
Expressions wrought in muted place,
Stillness breathes in crafted lines,
Sculpting silence where heart aligns.

Echoed void in sculptor's hand,
Shapes the form with silent command,
Timeless art in stillness cast,
Sculpting silence until the last.

Fathoms of Innovation

In depths unseen by mortal eyes,
Where thoughts like quicksilver arise,
We venture forth through boundless seas,
And harvest from the mind's vast trees.

Each wave an idea, each crest a spark,
Innovation's journey through the dark,
From shadows bright inventions spring,
Their melodies of future sing.

Diving deep in curious quest,
A sinking mind finds needed rest,
And from the ocean's floor of dreams,
Emerge solutions, endless streams.

With every stroke, the waters part,
Unveiling new forms of art,
Exploration without end,
In innovation's arms, we bend.

The fathoms call us, beckon near,
Where foresight casts away all fear,
In deepest blue, we carve our way,
To forge tomorrow from today.

Celestial Creations

Upon the canvas of the night,
Stars paint their tales with beams of light,
In whispered constellations weave,
A story only dreams conceive.

Galaxies in spiral dance,
A cosmic edge in vast expanse,
Nebulae in colors blend,
A universe that knows no end.

Comets burst in fleeting blaze,
Through the silence, through the haze,
Sculpting patterns, tracing lines,
In the dark, their beauty shines.

Planetary waltz so grand,
In this celestial wonderland,
Orbits drawn by gravity's thread,
Where mortal foot has never tread.

Each twilight sky a newborn chart,
The universe in every heart,
Celestial dreams ignite the night,
With endless worlds of pure delight.

Muse's Playground

In fields where inspiration blooms,
And muses dance through floral rooms,
Ideas sprung from fertile ground,
In colors, shapes, and dreams unbound.

The playground of a restless mind,
Where errant thoughts are gently kind,
Creativity in joyful play,
That brings forth light to every day.

Across the swaying grassy blades,
In shadows cast and hidden glades,
The muse's hand guides every brush,
In vibrant scenes without the rush.

Ephemeral and ever bright,
In the canvasses of night,
Songs of heart and whispers loud,
Emerge from inspiration's shroud.

Here in the muse's sacred land,
Creation crafted by each hand,
In endless bounds of thought and feel,
Our inner world's most pure appeal.

Artistic Odyssey

Embark upon a ship of dreams,
On currents where emotion streams,
A voyage through the artist's sea,
To realms where only passion see.

Each stroke a compass, each hue a guide,
Through stormy waves and shifting tide,
With canvas sails and brush in hand,
We navigate life's vast command.

In every scene, a story told,
In colors bright or shadows bold,
An odyssey through time and space,
With art's embrace, we find our place.

Through landscapes vast and still untold,
Our visions glimmer, soft yet bold,
A journey where the heart's decree,
Transforms the world that we can see.

Upon this artistic, boundless quest,
Creativity our soul's bequest,
With every step and every line,
An odyssey, forever thine.

Fragments of Genius

In shards of light, the mind does soar,
Through tangled paths, it finds the core.
A spark ignites, the magic flows,
In brilliant glimpses, genius shows.

Puzzle pieces, scattered wide,
Together form a truth inside.
Mirrors of thought, reflections gleam,
In fractured visions, we dream.

Flashes of brilliance in the night,
Illuminate the chosen sight.
A fleeting glimpse of something grand,
Held only in a fragile hand.

Fragments weave a tapestry,
Of ideas, wild and free.
The broken parts, when stitched as one,
Reveal the work that's never done.

In whispers soft, the genius speaks,
Through broken lines, the truth it seeks.
United by the common thread,
Forever in the mind, it's fed.

Shaping the Void

From emptiness, creation grows,
In silent space, the vision flows.
With every stroke, the void takes form,
An artist's touch, in chaos warm.

Infinite dark, a canvas wide,
A mind's eye sees what it will hide.
With patient hand, and steady heart,
The void becomes the greatest art.

Shapes emerge from nothingness,
Crafted with a deep finesse.
A universe within the mind,
In silence, wisdom we can find.

Sculpting truths from shapeless dreams,
In every line, a story teems.
With focused thought, the void is shaped,
A masterpiece, at last escaped.

In the shadows, light does creep,
Awakening the depths we keep.
The void transformed by intent,
A mark of what the heart has meant.

Whispers of Vision

In twilight's hush, the whispers start,
Secrets born within the heart.
A vision forms, elusive, clear,
A voice that only dreamers hear.

Through corridors of mind it sweeps,
A silent call from depths it keeps.
A gentle nudge, a soft command,
A guiding force, a steady hand.

Phantoms of thought in shadow play,
Reveal the path, show the way.
Their murmurs weave a silken thread,
Connecting dreams to what lies ahead.

With eyes closed tight and spirit free,
We traverse realms we cannot see.
The whispers guide with subtle grace,
To places time will not erase.

In quiet moments, they will rise,
Reflections in our inward skies.
A vision whispered, fragile, true,
A gift that's meant for only you.

Imprints of Creativity

Upon a blank and empty page,
The artist frees imagination's cage.
With every stroke, a world appears,
Built from dreams, and subtle fears.

Colors blend, and lines entwine,
A map of thought, both bold and fine.
In every detail, essence gleams,
A symphony of fleeting dreams.

Hands that shape and minds that mold,
Stories waiting to be told.
Ephemeral, yet set in time,
Creativity transcends the climb.

Through every mark, a soul expressed,
By shadows touched, by light caressed.
The canvas holds a whispered trace,
Of journeys vast, of inner space.

And though the world may fade away,
In every work, memories stay.
Imprints left by fleeting thought,
The legacy that change has brought.

Fusion of Fantasies

In a realm where dreams collide,
Two worlds knit side by side,
Colors merge in endless flow,
In this place, our visions grow.

Whispers of forgotten tales,
Echo through the silent vales,
Magic dancing in the air,
Fusing truths beyond compare.

Starlit pathways weave and wane,
Guiding hearts through joy and pain,
Boundless realms of hope and lore,
Unlocking ever more.

Mysteries in twilight haze,
Unraveling in brilliant craze,
Bound by threads of pure belief,
A tapestry of shared relief.

Here in fusion's vibrant glow,
Strangers meet and dare to know,
Beauty born of wild minds,
Fantastical scenes intertwined.

Nebula of Notions

In cosmic clouds of thought we drift,
A nebula where ideas lift,
Stars of insight, shining bright,
Guiding through the endless night.

Concepts bloom in spectral hues,
Merging, mingling like the dews,
Infinite in form and flight,
In this realm of pure delight.

Winds of wisdom softly blow,
Through the nebula we flow,
Galaxies of notions wide,
In their depths, we gently glide.

Boundless dreams and notions blend,
Aliens to an earthly end,
In this space of boundless mind,
Our greatest truths we surely find.

Threads of thought in cosmic scheme,
Woven into every dream,
In the nebula's warm embrace,
Notions find their rightful place.

Shaping Dreams

Sculpting realms from misty strands,
With the finest of command,
Dreams take shape in twilight's glow,
Within our hearts, they grow.

Chiseling hopes with tender flair,
Crafting visions from the air,
Molding futures, soft and bright,
Through the canvas of the night.

Hammering stars with gentle care,
Forging paths beyond compare,
Dreams that shimmer, dreams that shine,
Crafted from a power divine.

In our hands, we hold the clay,
Shaping what tomorrow may,
Boundless forms in slumber's cloak,
At the dawn, new life evoke.

Building worlds from whispered sights,
We ignite the darkest nights,
Painting dreams with vibrant beams,
Creating life from fleeting dreams.

Inventive Waves

Waves of thought, relentless, vast,
Crashing through the mind, so fast,
Ideas swell in vibrant throng,
In their pulse, we find our song.

Currents of creation surge,
Through the waves, new concepts urge,
Riding crests of purest light,
Inspiration day and night.

Swells of genius break the shore,
Unveiling treasures to explore,
From the deep, invention springs,
On these waves, the future clings.

Ebb and flow of novel dreams,
Ripples turning into streams,
In the tide, our visions float,
Wave on wave, creation's boat.

Rolling forth on mind's expanse,
Waves of thought in endless dance,
In their motion, art and lore,
Ride the waves forevermore.

Crafting Realities

Through thought we weave the canvas bright,
A tapestry of day and night.
In shadows deep, and sunlight clear,
We craft the world both far and near.

With hands that mold the clay of dreams,
And hearts that pulse with silent screams.
We build from fragments, bold and free,
A realm where all our visions see.

In every stroke, the colors blend,
A symphony that has no end.
We sketch the stars, we paint the moon,
Crafting realities in a silent tune.

The brush of fate within our grasp,
Unveils the truths we dare to clasp.
We shape the realms in which we live,
And in this act, our souls we give.

Labyrinth of Ideas

Within the mind, a maze unfolds,
A labyrinth where thought takes hold.
Each corridor, a twist of fate,
A passageway to contemplate.

Ideas bloom in cryptic halls,
Upon the mind's internal walls.
With steps uncertain, paths we trace,
In search of wisdom's hidden grace.

Through winding routes of hope and fear,
We navigate what isn't clear.
A mental quest, a race unfurled,
In the endless maze of the inner world.

The labyrinth yields no easy key,
Just endless realms of thought to see.
We wander through, both lost and found,
In the vast ideas that here abound.

Introspection Artistry

With inward gaze, the art begins,
A canvas where the soul unpins.
Each stroke reveals the inner sight,
In hues of darkness, shades of light.

The artist's hand, both firm and true,
Sketches what the mind construes.
In shadowed lines, in colors bold,
The silent tales of self unfold.

Layers deep, yet lightly placed,
An introspective work embraced.
Each detail tells a story known,
Of fears, and hopes, and dreams alone.

Inward realms of endless depth,
A personal mosaic deftly kept.
Introspection's artistry,
Reveals the depths of our true sea.

Ingenious Moments

Ephemeral, the thought arrives,
A spark within our conscious dives.
The fleeting flash of insight clear,
Ingenious moments we revere.

In seconds brief, the ideas form,
A mental storm, both bright and warm.
A burst of brilliance from the air,
Creativity beyond compare.

These moments swift, like lightning's blaze,
Illuminate our mental maze.
Solutions come with sudden grace,
Brightening thoughts that interlace.

Ingenious moments, bold and swift,
A timeless mental, precious gift.
A flash that changes all we see,
And shapes the future yet to be.

Milton Keynes UK
Ingram Content Group UK Ltd.
UKHW022248080824
446595UK00003B/70

9 789916 763803